The Song of Eros

The Song of Eros

ANCIENT GREEK LOVE POEMS

Translated by Bradley P. Nystrom

Illustrated by Claudette Sherbert Little

Southern Illinois University Press

Carbondale

12 11 10 09   4 3 2 1

Designed by Edward D. King

Library of Congress Cataloging-in-Publication Data
    The Song of Eros: ancient Greek love poems / translated by Bradley P.
    Nystrom; illustrated by Claudette Sherbert Little.
        p. cm.

    1. Love poetry, Greek—Translations into English. 2. Love poetry,
English—Translations from Greek. I. Nystrom, Bradley P.
PA 3624.L7S6 1991   90-35758
881'.0108354—dc20   CIP
ISBN-13: 978-0-8093-1640-3 (cloth : alk. paper)
ISBN-10: 0-8093-1640-4 (cloth : alk. paper)
ISBN-13: 978-0-8093-2906-9 (pbk. : alk. paper)
ISBN-10: 0-8093-2906-9 (pbk.: alk. paper)

The paper used in this publication meets the minimum requirements of
American National Standard for Information Sciences—Permanence of
Paper for Printed Library Materials, ANSI Z39.48-1992. ⊚

For Jennifer

Contents

PREFACE

FOR most people Greek poetry means Homer, and
rightly so, since the first and greatest of Greek poets is
that singer of tales of men at arms and a hero's return
home from Troy. But there were also those who sang of
love, artists who celebrated in verse the whole range of
experience and emotion that every lover knows. Love,
hate, suspicion, infatuation, rejection, ecstasy—the
poets knew them well, and so there is much that is fa-
miliar in their poems. We may even find there, looking
back across the centuries, glimpses of ourselves in lives
lived long ago.

The poems in this book span the period from the
Archaic Age to the beginning of the Byzantine era, that
is, from the seventh century B.C. to the sixth century
A.D. The earliest, some of which are only fragments, are
the works of the early iambic and elegiac poet Archi-
lochos and the lyric poets Sappho and Anakreon. The
rest belong to the *Greek Anthology*, a collection of
slightly more than four thousand epigrams compiled in
the tenth century by the Byzantine scholar Kephalas.
Although they shared a common language, not all of

the poets were from Greece; among them were residents of Italy, Egypt, Syria, Macedonia, and Lydia. That they wrote in Greek and accepted its poetic norms is testimony to the immense influence of Greek civilization throughout the ancient Mediterranean world.

I have tried to preserve as much as possible of the clarity, conciseness, insight, and wit that distinguish these poems in the original Greek. If these shine through in translation we must give the credit to the poets, who crafted their poems with a skill that has enabled them to survive the sometimes ungentle hand of the translator.

I want to thank my friends and colleagues Noie Koehler and Richard Cooper for their interest in the poems and the helpful advice they offered as I worked on the translations. My good friend and teacher, Professor Stylianos Spyridakis of the University of California at Davis, gave me encouragement just when it was needed. Finally, my wife, Jennifer, read the translations in many stages of revision and made useful suggestions for their improvement.

The Song of Eros

MELEAGROS

1 ·

In the name of Love,
I swear that I would rather hear
Heliodora's whisper in my ear
than the shining harp of Apollo.

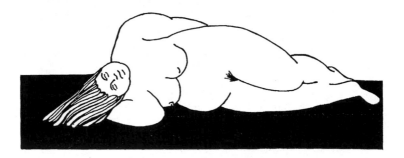

SAPPHO

2

The moon is down,
and the Pleiades.
It's midnight,
time passes,
and I lie alone.

MELEAGROS

3

I will plait white violets,
myrtle, and soft narcissus too.
I will twine laughing lilies
and sweet crocus, purple hyacinths,
and the roses lovers cherish,
so the wreath I set
on lovely Heliodora's brow
will scatter petals on her scented hair.

DIONYSIOS SOPHISTES

4

Hello there, rose girl,
you have a rosy charm.
But what are you selling?
Yourself?
Your roses?
Both?

ASKLEPIADES

5

Wine is the test for love:
Nikagoras told us he loved no one,
but his many toasts betrayed him.
Oh yes! He bent his head and wept,
and then his wreath slipped,
half to cover the aching in those
sad dark eyes.

STRATON

6

If my kiss offends you
then punish me with yours.

POSEIDIPPOS

7

If someone's with her, I'll go,
but if she's sleeping alone
then for God's sake give me
just a moment inside.
Tell her I'm drunk, that I've made my way
past thugs and thieves to her door.
Tell her reckless Love was my guide.

KRINAGORAS

8

Tossing, turning, back and forth,
all night long on your empty bed.
Poor Krinagoras: you'll get no sleep
till lovely Gemella lies by your side.

SAPPHO

9

Don't try to bend a stubborn heart.

10

When you were a green grape you refused me.
When you were ripe in the bunch you sent me away.
Give me, at least, a bite of your raisin.

Anonymous

ASKLEPIADES

11

This tomb holds Archeanassa,
the courtesan from Kolophon
whose very wrinkles were graced
by sweet Love.
Oh you lovers who gathered
the fresh blossoms of her youth,
what a fire you passed through!

RUFINUS

12

Melite,
you have Hera's eyes,
Athena's hands,
Aphrodite's breasts
and Thetis' feet.
Happy is the man who sees you,
thrice-blessed is he who hears your voice,
the one who kisses you finds paradise
and he who marries you is a god.

ASKLEPIADES

13

Sweet for the thirsty
is a drink of snow in summer,
and sweet for sailors to run before
spring breezes at winter's end.
But sweeter still is the single cloak
that hides two lovers as they honor Aphrodite.

MARCUS ARGENTARIUS

14

There is more to love than finding
someone beautiful to please your critical eye.
This is love, this is fire:
delighting in someone less than lovely
and adoring her with a heart aflame.
Anyone can like a pretty face.

BIANOR

15

I'm a nobody,
no one special,
a nothing—
yet even I am loved.
Even I am the master
of someone else's soul.

EUENOS

16

If hating is pain and loving is pain,
then of these two bitter agonies
give me the one that's bittersweet.

RUFINUS

17

I love everything about you—
everything but that wandering eye of yours,
so fond of the most vile of men.

ARCHILOCHOS

18

Such was my passion for love
that it twisted itself beneath my heart
and spread thick mist across my eyes,
stealing my tender wits away.

MARCUS ARGENTARIUS

19

Melissa, you're the image of your namesake,
the flower-loving honeybee.
I know this woman, and I take it to heart.
You kiss me, and your lips are honey.
You ask for money, and I am stung.

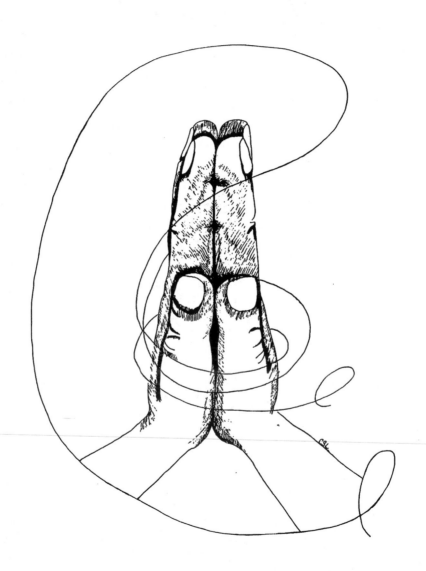

PAULUS SILENTIARIUS

20

Doris drew a single strand from her golden hair
and bound my hands, making me her prisoner.
At first I laughed, thinking I would easily
shake off the lovely girl's ties,
but when I had no strength to break them
I groaned, like one held fast by brazen bonds.
And now, the most miserable of men,
I hang on a hair, following my mistress
wherever she wishes to drag me.

PAULUS SILENTIARIUS

21

Delectable Theano came to stay with me,
but she wept bitter tears all night long
and cursed the rising evening star
for pointing to the coming dawn.
We mortals are never satisfied.
We lovers must have dawnless nights.

MELEAGROS

22

Oh moody morning star,
why have you chosen this,
of all nights, to dawdle in your
great spin around the world?
Why tonight, when another lies
warm and snug beneath my Demo's cloak?
And why, when my slender love lay with me,
did you come so soon to bring the light
and laugh to end our tender night?

RUFINUS

23

Seeing Prodike alone and happy,
I clasped her sweet knees and begged:
Save a man who's nearly lost!
Let me have what little life I've got!
She wept as I spoke,
but then she wiped away her tears
and with gentle hands pushed me away.

SAPPHO

24

Love shook my heart
like wind pounding mountain oaks.

MELEAGROS

25

My wine cup's laughing, giggling,
slipped between the sweet sipping
lips of Zenophila,
the girl who loves to love.
Lucky cup! If only she would
bring her mouth to mine and with
one breath drink down my very soul.

MELEAGROS

26

Tender Asklepias has clear blue eyes,
gentle seas inviting us to set sail for love.

RUFINUS

27

Here, Rhodoklea, is a garland,
blossoms laced by my own hands.
Here are lilies and roses,
moist anemones, soft narcissus
and dark-gleaming violets.
Wear them, and cease to be vain.
Your beauty, like theirs, will fade.

RUFINUS

28

Let's you and me jump
into the bath together, Prodike.
We'll crown ourselves with garlands
and drink our fill of unmixed wine.
Our time for rejoicing is short:
soon we're old, then we're dead.

AGATHIAS

29

Why are you sighing?

    I'm in love.

With whom?

    A girl.

Is she pretty?

    Oh yes!

Where did you meet her?

    At a dinner party.

Do you think you have a chance with her?

    I know I do, friend, but I want it kept secret.

Ah, so you don't plan to marry her?

    No, I've learned she's penniless.

What? Liar! You don't love her!

How can a heart in love make calculations?

PHILODEMOS

30

Xanthippe's
touch upon the lyre,
her playful speech,
her inviting eyes,
her singing
and the fire they have set
will burn you.
Why and when and how
I cannot say,
but they will,
poor heart,
they will.

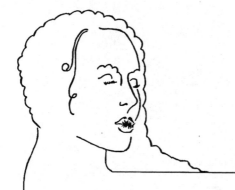

31

A girl kissed me in the
early evening with wet lips.
Her kiss was nectar,
her mouth divine.
And now I am drunk with the kiss,
for I have drunk deeply of love.

Anonymous

MELEAGROS

32

Hardhearted Eros,
if you burn my little soul
too often she will fly away.
She has wings too.

33

She who sets whole towns on fire,
Sthenelais, the high-priced girl
who pours herself like gold over
those with coin to buy her,
lay naked beside me all last night,
giving me all I wanted and more
(and for free!) till dawn came
and the end of my dream.
Never again will I grovel before
her cruel beauty, nor sit and weep alone,
for now I find my pleasure in sensual sleep.

Anonymous

RUFINUS

34

I've armed myself with Logic against Love,
and if it's one on one he doesn't have a chance:
I, a mortal, will stand against a god!
But if he has Bacchus on his side
it's two against one, and I won't have a prayer.

DIOPHANES OF MYRINA

35

Eros is like a thief:
sharp-eyed, bold,
he robs us blind.

MELEAGROS

36

Eros, still a babe
in his mother's lap,
played at dice one morning
and tossed away my soul.

MELEAGROS

37

This Love I have inside me
is fond of playing ball,
and to you, Heliodora, he
throws my trembling heart,
saying, "catch!"
Please play with him,
Heliodora, and don't drop me;
he has no patience with those
who break the rules.

38

Lamplight only darkens the night
of a man cursed with an ugly wife.

39

I send you sweet perfume,
but more for its pleasure
than for yours:
you perfume perfume.

Anonymous

PLATO

40

My soul was on my lips
while I was kissing Agathon.
Wild thing! She came there
hoping to sneak across to him.

MELEAGROS

41

Give her my message, Dorkas.
Pay attention!
Be sure to repeat it twice,
no, three times.
Yes, Dorkas, the whole thing!
All right, get going—hurry!
Hey Dorkas, wait.
Wait a second! Stop!
Where are you going, Dorkas?
I haven't finished yet;
there's something else that . . .
(I'm such an idiot!)
never mind, don't say anything at all.
No wait, tell her everything.
Dorkas, why am I sending you, anyway?
Look, I'm going with you,
I mean, step aside, Dorkas,
I'll lead the way.

MELEAGROS

42

Cupbearer!
Fill our cups, and with each ladle
say again and again "to Heliodora!"
till the wine's mixed with her name,
and crown me with the wreath she wore
last night, a scented memory of her.
But look! The rose is weeping,
for it knows tonight she's sleeping
in someone else's arms.

PLATO

43

You're my Star, a stargazer too,
and I wish that I were Heaven,
with a billion eyes to look at you!

PHILODEMOS

44

I want no more white violets
and lyre-song,
no more Chian wines
and Syrian myrrh,
no more carousing
and drunken whores —
I hate them all,
they're driving me mad.
But wreathe me in narcissus
and let me taste the cross flute,
rub me down with saffron balm,
moisten my tongue with wine from Mytilene
and wed me to a hearth-and-home girl.

PHILODEMOS

45

Oh feet,
Oh legs,
Oh thighs I die for,
Oh bottom,
Oh mound,
Oh flanks,
Oh shoulders,
Oh breasts,
Oh slender neck,
Oh hands,
Oh eyes that drive me mad,
Oh skillful moves,
Oh exquisite tongue,
Oh inspiring moans.
Yes, her name is Flora and she *is* Italian.
And no, she cannot sing Sappho's Greek.
Yet Perseus loved Andromeda, and she was Indian!

MELEAGROS

46

Timarion's
kisses sting,
his eyes are fire,
his glances sear,
his touch inspires.

MELEAGROS

47

Even winged Eros
himself is stricken
(and in midair!)ˇ
a victim of your eyes,
Timarion.

ANAKREON

48

Look!
Climbing this
steep
white
crag
I turn and
leap

·

·

·

(drunk with love)

·

·

·

into
the
foaming
surf
below.

MELEAGROS

49

Heavy-laden ocean ships
cruising down the Hellespont,
sails full of the good North Wind,
if you should see Phanion
on the beach at Kos
gazing out upon the blue sea
tell her that love carries me there,
though not on shipboard, but by land.
Tell her, good ships,
and Zeus will breathe the fair wind
of his affection into your broad sails.

MELEAGROS

50

Shrill mosquitoes,
shameless bloodsuckers,
winged monsters of the night,
please, I beg you: let my
Zenophila sleep a while in peace,
and come gorge yourselves on me instead.
But what's the use of begging?
Even you relentless insects
delight in the soft warmth of her body.
Still, I'm warning you, you nasty bugs:
either stop your biting or you will feel
the smack of my jealous hands.

PAULUS SILENTIARIUS

51

They say a man bitten by a
mad dog sees the beast's image
reflected on the water.
I wonder: did Eros, rabid,
sink his bitter fangs in me?
I see you in the ocean deep,
the swirling stream
and the wine cup.

ANAKREON

52

I love, and I do not love.
I am mad, and I am not mad.

ANTIPHILOS

53

Hey beautiful! Wait up!

What's your name, honey?

When can I see you again?

We'll do whatever you like.

Hey, don't you speak?

Where do you live?

I'll have a slave see you home.

You're not attached, are you?

Not talking?

Well, goodbye then, you stuck-up girl.

Won't you even say goodbye?

It doesn't matter, I'll be back.

I know how to soften a heart like yours.

But for now, baby, goodbye.

MARCUS ARGENTARIUS

54

You had love, Sosikrates,
when you had money,
but now that you are poor it seems
there's no love left for you.
What a cure for love is poverty!
Even Menophila, who used to call you
her cutie and her darling Adonis,
now asks who you are and where you're from.
I guess you've had to learn the meaning
of that old saying:
"The man who has nothing has nobody
for a friend."

PALLADAS OF ALEXANDRIA

55

Zenon, war has broken out in your house
because you married the daughter of
Protomachos (first in a fight)
and Nikomache (victorious in a fight).
What you need is a helpful adulterer,
a Lysimachos (deliverer from a fight)
who will take pity on you and
deliver you from Andromache (man-fighter),
the daughter of Protomachos

MELEAGROS

56

It must have been Eros himself
who sharpened Heliodora's fingernail;
even her gentlest love-scratching
pierces my heart.

ASKLEPIADES

57

The night is long and wintry.

The Pleiades glimmer in the chilling dark.

Back and forth before her door I pass,

soaking wet with rain and tormented

by desire for her—the cheater.

This can't be love! No!

Aphrodite has shot me instead with agony,

a burning dart straight from the fire.

SAPPHO

58

You came, and I was longing for you.
You cooled a heart that burned with desire.

ASKLEPIADES

59

Didyme waved a twig at me
and I was swept away.
Even now, gazing upon her beauty,
I melt like wax before the fire.
Yes, her skin is dark and foreign,
but what is that to me?
The coals, too, are dark,
but when we light them
they shine as brightly as roses.

POSEIDIPPOS

60

Don't think you can fool me
with those crocodile tears, Philainis.
I know the truth:
As long as you're lying beside me
you say there's no one you love more,
but if you were with someone else
you'd say you love him more than me.

LEONTIOS

61

Oh cup, touch her honeyed lips.
Taste them while you have the chance.
And know I don't begrudge your pleasure,
I only wish I had your luck.

62

I wish I were the wind, and
that you, walking on the shore,
would bare your breasts
and take me to them as I blow.

Anonymous

RUFINUS

63

The silver-toed girl was bathing,
letting the water splash and play
upon the golden apples of her breasts,
skin silky smooth as milk.
The round cheeks of her bottom
gently rolled and tossed together
as she turned and moved,
flesh more fluid than the water
that coursed down to where
her fingers spread to cover
the swelling flow—not all of it,
but as much as she could.

KRINAGORAS

64

Roses used to bloom in springtime,
but now in deepest winter
we burst into scarlet,
smiling on your birthday morn
and soon your wedding day as well.
Better to crown the loveliest of women
than to wait for spring and sun.

RUFINUS

65

Europa's kiss would be sweet
resting lightly on the lips,
the faintest touch upon the mouth.
But more, much more than this:
she presses close and hard
and pulls the soul up from my fingertips.

MACEDONIUS

66

Every year the harvesters
gather in the vintage,
and not one frowns on the
vines' curling tendrils.
I too am a harvester,
holding rosy-armed you entwined
in the supple knot of my embrace
and gathering in the vintage of love.
No better summer, no other spring
could ever be, for it's now that
you are young and full of every joy,
and I pray that you will stay
this way forever.
But if some wrinkle like a tendril
comes creeping, I will scarcely blink,
because I love you.

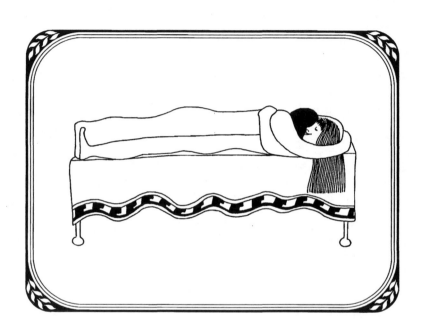

MARCUS ARGENTARIUS

67

Diokleia, you'll see, is thin,
a skinny Aphrodite, though she
has the most delightful ways.

Then not much will come between us.
I'll fall upon her little chest
and lie as close as may be to her soul.

68

I fell for her,
I kissed her,
I was lucky,
I am loved.
But who I am,
and who she is,
and how it happened,
God only knows.

Anonymous

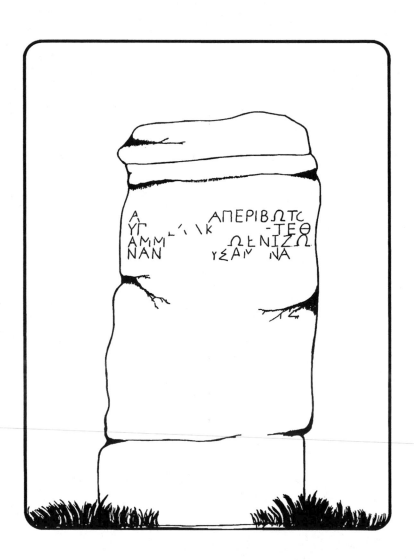

69

Here, beneath this stone, I lie,
the famous woman who shed her clothes
for only one man.

Anonymous

70

I feel like a god,
sitting so close to you,
listening intently to your
gentle voice and sweet laughter.
I hear you, and my heart
trembles in my breast.
I see you, and I can no longer
speak;
my tongue has snapped, and
a thin quick fire runs beneath
my skin. My eyes are empty,
my ears hum, and
I am covered with sweat.
I shiver, pale as summer grass,
and feel myself slip
close to the edge of death.

SAPPHO

71

Happy bridegroom!
The wedding you hoped for
has happened;
the maiden you prayed for
is yours!

72

All I want is to
touch Neoboule's hand.

73

A grammarian's daughter made love with a man
and bore a child masculine, feminine, and neuter.

SAPPHO

74

Some say a host of horsemen,
others a troop of infantry,
others still a fleet of ships
is the fairest sight on the dark earth.
But I say it is the one you love.
And this is easily proved,
for Helen, the most beautiful of women,
sailed off to Troy without a thought
for her child and kin,
thinking of her beloved alone.
I think of Anaktoria, who is far away,
for I would rather see her gentle step
and the glad radiance of her face
than all the chariots and armed men of Lydia.

LUCILIUS

75

Eutychos the painter produced twenty sons
and never got a single likeness.

MELEAGROS

76

Marathonis laid Nikopolis
in this stone tomb,
wetting the marble with tears
that fell in vain:
Only sorrow remains
when a man's wife is gone.

MELEAGROS

77

My soul warns me to run from Heliodora,
the cause of my past hurts and tears.
She begs me to flee, but I cannot bring
myself to leave.
The shameless girl herself says I should go,
but all the while she covers me with kisses.

RUFINUS

78

I used to pray, Thalia,
for the night when you would come
and I would satisfy my longing
with armfuls of luscious you.
And now you are here,
naked and willing beside me,
but I am loose and limp with sleep.
Wake up, body!
How can you do this to me?
I may never have this chance again!

AGATHIAS

79

Anxious to learn if fair-eyed Ereutho
really loved me, I tested her heart
with a clever ploy:
"I'm leaving," I said, "for a far-off land,
but you must stay behind, my darling,
faithful to me and our love until
at last I return."
Then, crying out, she leaped up, struck
her face with her fists, tore her curls,
and begged me stay until, like one
not easily persuaded, and with a
disappointed look, I gave in to her.
Now I am happy in my love,
for I have the thing I most wanted,
and by granting it as a favor too!

SAPPHO

80

You make me burn.

The Poets

AGATHIAS

Born in Myrina on the west coast of Asia Minor, Agathias lived from 536 to 582 A.D. He studied law in Alexandria and Constantinople, where he earned the title *scholastikos,* and edited an anthology of poems that became the basis of the *Greek Anthology.*

ANAKREON

Born in Teos in Asia Minor ca. 572 B.C., he spent much of the latter part of his life in Athens. One of the most important and influential of early Greek poets, he wrote six books of poetry.

ANTIPHILOS

A citizen of Byzantium, he was born late in the first century B.C. Antiphilos specialized in writing epigrams and contributed some fifty poems to the *Greek Anthology.*

ARCHILOCHOS

Archilochos was an iambic and elegiac poet from Paros who appears to have been born late in the eighth century B.C. Legend says the nobleman Lykambes promised him his daughter, Neoboule, but then reneged. Archilochos took his revenge by writing such effective satirical poems about Lykambes and his family that they eventually committed suicide.

ASKLEPIADES

A poet from Samos who flourished in the early part of the third century B.C.

BIANOR

Bianor was born in Bithynia in Asia Minor late in the first century B.C. Twenty-two poems are attributed to him.

DIONYSIOS SOPHISTES

Nothing is known of the poet but his name.

DIOPHANES OF MYRINA

An unknown poet of uncertain date.

EUENOS

There were several unknown poets who shared this name. Together, they produced eleven epigrams.

KRINAGORAS

Krinagoras of Mytilene was born ca. 70 B.C. He wrote
fifty-one poems.

LEONTIOS

A poet of the sixth century A.D., he wrote twenty-four
epigrams.

LUCILIUS

A poet of the first century A.D., Lucilius was patronized
by Nero and was the author of over one hundred twen-
ty poems. He was a humorist whose epigrams are nota-
ble for their extravagant hyperbole.

MACEDONIUS

The author of forty-four poems in the *Greek Anthol-
ogy*, Macedonius held the honorary title of consul dur-
ing the reign of Justinian in the sixth century A.D.

MARCUS ARGENTARIUS

A poet of the first century A.D., he wrote lively, elegant
epigrams. Thirty-seven of these are extant.

MELEAGROS

Born in Gadara ca. 140 B.C., Meleagros spent his youth in Tyre and his adult life on Kos. He wrote more than one hundred thirty epigrams, most of them erotic. Meleagros' collection of epigrams, the so-called *Garland* of Meleagros, was one of the first serious attempts to compile a critical anthology of Greek poems.

PALLADAS OF ALEXANDRIA

A poet and a teacher of literature, Palladas of Alexandria flourished at the end of the fourth century A.D. He wrote 150 poems included in the *Greek Anthology*.

PAULUS SILENTIARIUS

Paulus, entitled *Silentiarius* ("private secretary"), was a high official in the court of Justinian ca. 560 A.D. Eighty of his epigrams, about half of them erotic, are included in the *Greek Anthology*.

PHILODEMOS

A poet of the first century B.C., Philodemos was an Epicurean philosopher and occasional associate of such Roman notables as Cicero, Virgil, and Horace. Twenty-five of his epigrams survive in the *Greek Anthology*.

PLATO
The great Athenian philosopher is said to have written poems as a youth in the last years of the fifth century B.C. Only a few of these survive, but their merit has been recognized by authorities as great as Shelley.

POSEIDIPPOS
The author of about twenty extant poems, Poseidippos was born in the Macedonian city of Pella ca. 310 B.C.

RUFINUS
A poet of uncertain date, Rufinus lived sometime during the first five centuries A.D. He was a writer of erotic verse.

SAPPHO
One of the most famous and influential of all Greek poets, she was the head of a sorority dedicated to the veneration of Aphrodite. Many of her poems, of which only fragments remain, were written in celebration of the marriages of the young girls who were members of this *thiasos*. Sappho was a resident of the island of Lesbos and flourished in the first part of the sixth century B.C.

STRATON

This poet from Sardis was active in the early part of the second century A.D. Almost one hundred poems are included in his collection of homosexual verse that later appeared as Book XII of the *Greek Anthology*.

Index to the
Greek Texts

Unless otherwise noted, the translations are based on the Greek text of the Loeb edition of the *Greek Anthology,* edited by W. R. Paton (Cambridge, MA: Harvard University Press, 1916–26), 5 vols.

Poem	Greek Texts
1	V.141
2	D. A. Campbell, ed., *Greek Lyric Poetry* (New York: St. Martin's Press, 1969), I.168B
3	V.147
4	V.81
5	XII.135
6	XII.188
7	V.213
8	V.119
9	J. M. Edmonds, tr., *Lyra Graeca,* 3 vols. (Cambridge, MA: Harvard University Press, 1928–40), I.93
10	V.304
11	VII.217
12	V.94
13	V.169
14	V.89
15	A. S. F. Gow and D. L. Page, *Greek Anthology: Hellenistic Epigrams,* 2 vols. (Cambridge University Press, 1965), XI.364
16	XII.172
17	V.284

Poem	Greek Texts
18	Ernst Diehl et al., *Anthologia Lyrica Graeca,* 3d ed. (Leipzig, 1949–), I.112
19	V.32
20	V.230
21	V.283
22	V.173
23	V.66
24	Campbell, I.47
25	V.171 ·
26	V.156
27	V.74
28	V.12
29	V.267
30	V.131
31	V.305
32	V.57
33	V.2
34	V.93
35	V.309
36	XII.47
37	V.214
38	XI.287
39	V.91
40	V.78
41	V.182
42	V.136
43	VII.669
44	XI.34

Poem	Greek Texts
73	IX.489
74	Edmonds, I.38
75	XI.215
76	VII.340
77	V.24
78	V.47
79	V.287
80	Edmonds, I.27

Bradley Nystrom holds a doctorate in ancient history from the University of California at Davis and teaches in the history and humanities departments at California State University, Sacramento. He is co-editor and translator of two anthologies of classical Greek and Latin texts and has published articles on the subject of Greek Christian epigraphy. Mr. Nystrom lives in Sacramento with his wife, Jennifer, and their daughters, Alyssa and Alexandra.